ignite

WINTER SPORTS

FIGURE SKATING

Claire Throp

Raintree

Chicago, Illinois

Edited by Adam Miller, Nancy Dickmann,
    and John-Paul Wilkins
Designed by Richard Parker and Ken Vail Graphic
    Design
Picture research by Elizabeth Alexander
Originated by Capstone Global Library Ltd
Production by Vicki Fitzgerald
Printed and bound in China by Leo Paper
    Products Ltd

17 16 15 14 13
10 9 8 7 6 5 4 3 2 1

**Library of Congress Cataloging-in-Publication
Data**
Throp, Claire.
  Figure skating / Claire Throp.—1st ed.
    p. cm.—(Winter sports)
  Includes bibliographical references and index.
  ISBN 978-1-4109-5450-3 (hb)—ISBN 978-1-4109-
5456-5 (pb)
1. Figure skating—Juvenile literature. I. Title.

GV850.4.T48 2013
796.91'2—dc23   2012042735

Acknowledgments
We would like to thank the following for
permission to reproduce photographs: Alamy
pp. 4 (© Eileen Langsley/Figure Skating), 7
(© Lebrecht Music and Arts Photo Library),
9 (© GL Archive), 15 (© Aflo Co. Ltd.), 16, 20,
22 bottom (© PCN Photography), 17 top (©
Eileen Langsley Olympic Images), 17 bottom (©
Jean-Yves Ruszniewski/TempSport), 21 (© Paul
J Sutton/PCN), 26 (© Bruno Bebert/epa), 27 (©
Sergei Ilnitsky/epa), 28 (© Reuters), 30 (© Peter
Schneider/epa), 31 (© Rick Rickman/NewSport),
35 (© Gerry Penny/epa), 39 (© Sampics), 12;
Getty Images pp. 5 (Dean Mouhtaropoulos), 6
(SuperStock), 8 (Archive Photos/Fotosearch),
13 (Frederic J. Brown/AFP), 19 (Franck Fife/AFP/
Getty Images), 29 (Matthew Stockman), 32
(Fabrice Coffrini/AFP), 33 (Brian Bahr), 36 (John
Lamb/Photographer's Choice), 37 (Henry Georgi/
All Canada Photos), 38 (Kazuhiro Nogi/AFP), 41
(Thomas Coex/AFP); Shutterstock pp. imprint
page (© Diego Barbieri), 10 (© Alina G), 11, 14, 24,
25 (© Olga Besnard), 18, 22 top, 23, 40 (© testing),
34 (© ID1974), 47 (© GoodMood Photo).

Design features reproduced with permission of
Shutterstock (© Apostrophe, © CHEN WS,
© Dudarev Mikhail, © graph, © Kittichai,
© Ilaszlo, © marussia, © nadi555, © Nicemonkey,
© Pakhnyushcha, © Robert Adrian Hillman,
© RoyStudio.eu, © Umberto Shtanzman).

Cover photo of Mirai Nagasu of the United
States during the Figure Skating Gala at the
2010 Olympic Winter Games, Vancouver, British
Columbia, reproduced with permission of Alamy
(© PCN Photography).

CONTENTS

An Artistic Sport...4

A History of Skating 6

Starting Out: Equipment 10

Training..12

Jumps, Spins, and Lifts 16

Singles 24

Pairs and Ice Dance 26

Marking...28

Preparing for Competitions 30

Major Events...32

Skating for Fun 36

Quiz.. 42

Glossary... 44

Find Out More... 46

Index.. 48

Some words are shown in bold, **like this**. You can find out what they mean by looking in the glossary.

AN ARTISTIC SPORT

Torvill and Dean are legends in the world of ice dance. Their perfect score in 1984 has never been repeated.

It is the 1984 Winter Olympics. Jayne Torvill and Christopher Dean have been leading the world with their stunning ice dance routines. Their **free skate** is danced to Ravel's *Boléro*. As they end their routine with a deliberate, dramatic fall to the ground, the audience erupts. The couple collects flowers from the ice and sees three sixes (the top mark available) come up for **technical merit**. Suddenly, gasps go around the arena. The routine has won a perfect 6.0 for artistic impression from every judge. The couple wins the gold medal.

Athletic ability, **artistry**, and grace are all on show in figure skating. Amazing jumps, **lifts**, and spins add excitement and awe. These are all only possible because of the grueling training carried out by skaters throughout the year. Figure skating is a spectacular but tough sport.

Skating disciplines

There are four main **disciplines** that come under the term *figure skating*: men's, women's, pairs, and ice dance. **Synchronized skating** and a team competition are the newest additions.

This book will look at the different types of figure skating. It will also focus on the major championships and some of the best-known skaters.

"Figure skating is a mixture of art and sport."

– *Katarina Witt, retired German figure skater*

No WAY!

The term *figure skating* comes from the patterns or figures traced on the ice by skaters. Skating figures, or set patterns, on the ice were part of competitive skating until 1990, when they were removed because TV audiences found them boring.

A HISTORY OF SKATING

Skating is one of the oldest sports in the world. The earliest written evidence of skating for fun comes from 1180. Twelfth-century writer William Fitzstephen wrote of young men in London, England, playing around on ice with lances and shields and people coming to watch. The Dutch used to skate from village to village along frozen canals in the 13th century. They were the ones to discover skating on **edges**, which allowed people to skate smoothly from one foot to the other and became known as the Dutch roll. However, speed skating was the focus of the Dutch, and it was the English who developed figure skating.

NO WAY!

Skates were originally made from the leg bones of large animals, such as deer or sheep. They were attached by straps to the person's shoe. Poles were used to help push the person along. This type of skate dates back about 3,000 years, and they were still in use in the 1100s.

"Over the Parke where first in my life, it became a great frost, [I] did see people sliding with their skeets, which is a very pretty art."

– Samuel Pepys, a writer who lived in London in the 1660s

Skating as a pastime

During the 1640s, England was in a state of political turmoil. It ended in the beheading of the king. The royal family left England for Holland out of fear of their lives. James, the future King James II, learned the Dutch roll. The royals brought this new pastime back to England when Charles II returned to the throne in 1660. It was mainly men who skated at this time.

NO WAY!

The first skating club was set up in Edinburgh, Scotland, in 1742.

North American influence

In 1850, American Edward Bushnell started making steel blades for skates, and this allowed more complicated movements on the ice. American Jackson Haines was the man who mixed skating with dance and helped to form the sport we know today. Before Haines came on the scene, the style of figure skating was quite stiff and formal and focused on tracing figures on the ice. This was known as the English style. In the 1860s, Haines **pioneered** what became known as the international style of skating, which was much more fluid and expressive. It gradually became more athletic, too.

These people are skating for fun in Central Park, New York City, in 1890.

Pioneer winter sports

The International Skating Union (ISU) is the oldest international organization in winter sports, founded in the Netherlands in 1892. Figure skating was one of the first sports to compete internationally. An international figure skating competition was held in Vienna, Austria, in 1882. Figure skating was also contested in the 1908 and 1920 Olympic Games, and it has been featured in every Winter Olympic Games since the first one in 1924. Ice dancing joined the official Olympic program in 1976, and a team skating competition will appear in the 2014 Winter Olympics.

Mr. and Mrs. Johnson of England were World Pairs champions in the early 1900s.

NO WAY!

In the 1902 World Championships, Florence "Madge" Syers from Great Britain won the silver medal. What makes this special was that the competition was usually men only! However, there was no rule to say women couldn't compete, so Syers took advantage. Not long afterward, a separate championship was set up for women. Syers won the first two Ladies World Championships in 1906 and 1907.

STARTING OUT: EQUIPMENT

While the first skates to be worn were made of leather and wood or animal bones, today's boots allow skaters to perform incredible athletic feats on the ice.

Boots

Skating boots are made of strong leather with steel blades screwed to the bottom. The boots have a wide padded tongue and a high back to give lots of support to the ankle. There is a block heel to help with balance, and the blade goes out beyond the back of the boot. This helps to prevent skaters from falling backward. There is a **toe pick** on the front of the blade that is used in takeoff for jumps and as the pivot point for spins.

Blades

The slightly curved blades must be sharpened regularly. The blade is sharpened to a "V" shape, so there are two edges known as the **inside** and **outside edge**. To protect the blades when walking off the ice, plastic guards are placed over them.

tongue

toe pick

blade

heel

Clothing

The outfits worn by skaters must be comfortable and stretchy. Freedom of movement is important. Even when practicing, skaters must think about clothing—anything loose could be dangerous, since it may get caught in a skate.

The ice rink

For figure skating, the ice rink should measure no more than 200 feet by 100 feet (60 meters by 30 meters). The ice must be between 26 and 28 degrees Fahrenheit (−3.3 and −2.2 degrees Celsius).

TESSA VIRTUE & SCOTT MUIR

Born: May 17, 1989, in London, Canada (Virtue); September 2, 1987, in London, Canada (Muir)

Nationality: Canadian

Started skating: 1995 (Virtue); 1990 (Muir)

Practice during skating season: 30 hours a week

Known for: Being the Olympic ice dance gold medal winners in 2010 and world champions in 2012

Interesting fact: They both love golf!

TRAINING

Figure skaters, like most athletes, have to spend many hours every day training hard in order to reach the top…and then stay there.

On ice and off ice

Many skaters practice skating for two to three hours a day and then do some off-ice work, too. Balance and **posture** are extremely important for skating, so ballet and Pilates classes are common to help improve core stability and flexibility. Plyometrics—skipping or jumping followed by shuttle runs—are useful for building up the explosive power needed to perform complicated jumps. Core strength is essential for balance and control of the upper body during jumps and spins. Top skaters may train off the ice five days a week.

To be able to spin so fast you are a blur on the ice, you need to have a strong core, great balance, and flexibility.

Healthy eating

All athletes need to eat healthy meals in order to take care of their bodies. Making sure that they have enough energy to successfully land a jump or complete a **combination** is essential. Drinking enough is also important. Dehydration can make muscles feel tired.

> "No amount of money or facilities is going to create a skating star. You have to have a skater who is dedicated, passionate, and willing to learn."
>
> – Robin Cousins, retired figure skater

Warming up the muscles helps to prevent injury, as does stretching the muscles after exercising.

NAIL-BITING MOMENT!

At the 1991 World Championships, Japanese figure skater Midori Ito finished fourth. However, it wasn't certain she would finish at all. During the warm-up, she ran into another competitor. If that wasn't bad enough, she then crashed off the ice and into a television camera as she attempted a combination jump. Was her competition over? No—she got back on the ice and continued skating!

The cost of training

Most skaters do not go straight to competing in national or international championships. Instead, they have to achieve certain levels of ability and then display this in many local and regional competitions. Amateur skaters do not get paid to perform their sport, so the cost of training can prevent some talented people from being able to compete.

Skaters and their families often have to be willing to sacrifice vacations, new cars, and other luxuries in order to establish themselves. Some skaters have been lucky enough to have help from people outside their family. American skater Todd Eldredge was helped by fund-raising events in Chatham, Massachusetts, his hometown. Later in his career, he gave money back to the town to help younger athletes there.

"In skating or any amateur sport, as athletes we share something in common: the cost of training is quite a burden on our parents or on the athletes themselves trying to find a way to pay for their costs."

– Patrick Chan, Canadian figure skater

Mental preparation

Athletes often talk about mental preparation being important for winning competitions, but what does this mean? Thinking positively, being confident, staying relaxed, being motivated, and wanting to win are some of the things that top skaters do to stay at their best.

NO WAY!

In 2008, Japanese skater Daisuke Takahashi performed his free skate to a hip-hop version of Tchaikovsky's classical ballet *Swan Lake*!

ASHLEY WAGNER

Born: May 16, 1991, in Heidelberg, Germany
Nationality: American
Started skating: 1996
Practice during skating season: 20 hours a week
Job: Student
Known for: 2012 Four Continents Champion
Interesting fact: Ashley hates bananas!

JUMPS, SPINS, AND LIFTS

Modern figure skating includes spectacular jumps, spins, lifts, and **throws**. Jumps are identified by the takeoff and the number of times the skater spins in the air during the jump, known as revolutions. A single jump is one that has only one revolution, while a quadruple (or "quad") has four.

Toe jump

With toe jumps, skaters use the toe pick on their skate to help them push off from the ice. The following are toe jumps:

- **Toe loop**: The skater glides backward and uses the toe pick on one foot to gain stability before pushing off from the back outside edge of the other foot, and then landing on that same back outside edge.

- **Flip**: In a toe-pick-assisted jump, the skater takes off from the back inside edge of one foot and lands on the back outside edge of the other foot.

- **Lutz**: In a toe-pick assisted jump, the skater glides backward and takes off from the back outside edge of one foot. He or she lands on the back outside edge of the other foot.

Edge jump

Edge jumps get their names because the skater takes off from the edge of one skate without using the other skate to help. These are the main edge jumps:

- **Axel**: This is the only jump where the skater takes off from his or her forward outside edge and lands on the back outside edge of the opposite foot.

- **Loop**: The skater takes off from the back outside edge and lands on the same back outside edge.

- **Salchow**: The skater takes off from the back inside edge of one foot and lands on the back outside edge of the other foot.

KURT BROWNING

Born: June 18, 1966, in Alberta, Canada

Nationality: Canadian

Started skating: 1969

Job: Commentator for major skating competitions for Canadian television

Known for: Landing the first quadruple jump (a toe loop) in a World Championship in 1988; winning the World Championships four times

Interesting fact: Kurt's father built a small ice rink outside their house, and that is where Kurt learned to skate!

Spins

Spins are performed either forward or backward and they should be centered, which means the skate stays in roughly the same place on the ice. There are three main types of spin:

- Upright spins: These are spins on one or both feet standing upright.

- **Sit spins**: These are spins carried out on one leg in a sitting position.

- Camel spins: These are performed on one leg, with the non-skating leg parallel to the ice.

Many variations on these spins exist, including the layback spin, where the skater arches his or her back to look at the ceiling while spinning. A combination spin is when a skater changes feet and position while spinning fast. A flying spin is when a spin starts with a jump.

NO WAY!

In 2006, Natalia Kanounnikova carried out a spin at a speed of 304.47 revolutions per minute. That's fast!

camel spin

Do skaters get dizzy?

Most skaters do feel dizzy when they come out of a spin, but after years of training, they get used to it. Skaters try to focus on a fixed point as they start a spin, in order to avoid feeling too dizzy.

The Biellmann spin is a variation on the layback, where the skater reaches over his or her head to grab the blade of the boot on the non-skating leg. World champion Swiss skater Denise Biellmann was the first person to do this spin. Here, Germany's Annette Dytrt performs the Biellmann spin during the European Figure Skating Championships of 2006.

NAIL-BITING MOMENT!

In the 1988 Winter Olympics, Katarina Witt (Germany) and Debi Thomas (United States) both chose different parts of Bizet's opera *Carmen* to skate to in their free skate. There was already a rivalry between these two skaters, but now it was the "Battle of the Carmens." Thomas was leading going into the free skate, but then she landed incorrectly from a jump and never got back to her best. Witt won gold, while Thomas took the bronze.

Throws

Pairs do two types of jumps: side-by-side jumps and throws. In side-by-side jumps, each skater does a solo jump, but has to take off at the same time as a partner. Throws are assisted jumps, where the man assists the woman so that she can jump higher.

In the twist lift, the man lifts the woman above his head and then throws her in the air. She rotates up to three times and is then caught at the waist and placed back on the ice.

NO WAY!

The first throw triple axel was landed by Americans Rena Inoue and John Baldwin in the 2006 Olympic Games.

Ice dance lifts

Both pairs and ice dancers do lifts, but in ice dance, the woman must not go above the man's shoulder. There are two types of dance lifts: the long lift, which can last for no more than twelve seconds, and the short lift, which can last for no more than six seconds, with many variations on each.

Pairs lifts

There are five different pairs lifts based on the type of hold: armpit, waist, hand to hip, and two hand-to-hand types, the lasso and the press. The most basic lift is the overhead lift, where the man holds the woman above his head with his arms stretched out. Another example is the star lift, where the man lifts the woman by her hips and she forms a star shape with her outstretched arms and legs and her head.

British pair Sinead and John Kerr perform a spectacular lift in the original dance at the World Figure Skating Championships in 2009.

Spirals

Spirals are similar to spins, but the skaters do not rotate on one spot. They glide forward or backward on one foot and hold their non-skating leg in the air behind them. Spirals can be done by single skaters or pairs.

death spiral

Unison

One of the main **elements** of both pairs and ice dance is moving in **unison**. There are two types: exact and mirror. In exact unison, skaters try to match the position, **turnout**, and height of their bodies, arms, and legs. In mirror unison, they do the mirror opposite of their partner.

Other ice dance moves

Ice dancers perform moves that stay closer to the ice, such as drapes, where the woman lies over the man's knee, and pull-throughs, where the man pulls the woman between his legs. These moves show the flexibility of the skaters.

WENJING SUI AND CONG HAN

Born: July 18, 1995, in Harbin, China (Sui); August 6, 1992, in Harbin, China (Han)

Nationality: Chinese

Started skating: 2001 (Sui); 1998 (Han)

Practice during skating season: 17 hours a week

Known for: Winning the Four Continents pairs competition in 2012 and being World Junior champions three times

Interesting fact: They started skating after seeing Xue Shen and Hongbo Zhao skating at the 2002 Winter Olympics.

SINGLES

Both individual men and women skaters have to perform a **short program**. This is followed by the free skate, also known as the long program.

The short program

The short program cannot last more than 2 minutes, 40 seconds, and it makes up one-third of the final score. It must include the eight elements required by all competitors. The elements can be performed in any order. The top 24 skaters go through to the free skate.

PATRICK CHAN

Born: December 31, 1990, in Ottawa, Canada
Nationality: Canadian
Started skating: 1996
Practice during skating season: 30 hours a week
Known for: Being 2011 and 2012 World Champion
Interesting fact: Patrick took lessons in figure skating to help him learn how to skate for ice hockey, but he liked it so much that he became a figure skater instead!

The free skate

The free skate should last no longer than four minutes for women and four-and-a-half minutes for men. The free skate makes up two-thirds of the final score. The skaters choose their own music, and the **choreography** is designed to show off their best skills.

Yu-Na Kim (pictured) is known as "Queen Kim" in her home country of South Korea. She is so well known that she was asked to join Pyeongchang's successful attempt to win the right to host the Winter Olympics of 2018.

Compulsory figures

Compulsory figures were based on different ways of tracing two or three circles into the ice. Until 1947, these figures made up 60 percent of a skater's marks. But with more and more skating being shown on television, there were calls to change this. Viewers found the compulsory section boring, so gradually the figures lost importance, until they were finally removed in 1990.

PAIRS AND ICE DANCE

ALIONA SAVCHENKO AND ROBIN SZOLKOWY

Born: January 19, 1984, in Kiev, Ukraine (Savchenko); July 14, 1979, in Greifswald, Germany (Szolkowy)

Nationality: German

Started skating: 1989 (Savchenko); 1983 (Szolkowy)

Practice during skating season: 21 hours a week

Known for: Winning their fourth world pairs title in 2012—only the fifth couple to win four

Interesting facts: Aliona designs the costumes for their routines; Robin loves motorcycles.

There are a number of differences between the pairs and ice dance competitions. However, both disciplines focus on moving in unison.

Pairs

The pairs have to carry out the same program as the individual skaters: the short program followed by the free skate. They have to include at least three different lifts in the free skate, and judges look at the way the couple mirrors each other's movements.

Ice dance

Ice dancing is sometimes described as ballroom dancing on ice. Skaters have to do complicated footwork based on the original ballroom dances. Their routines do not include jumps and include only certain lifts. There are limits on the amount of time the skaters are apart and on the distance between them.

Ice dancing includes a short dance and a free dance. The short dance includes a compulsory dance (called a pattern dance) that changes every year. Skaters can choose their own music and choreography for the free dance. They can choose music that includes vocals, whereas pairs can only use instrumental music. The free dance makes up 50 percent of their score. There are still some **required elements**, such as particular sequences of steps.

27

MARKING

In competitions, skaters try to perform as difficult a routine as they can in order to earn technical merit marks. They also need to present the routine as well as they can, which gains them **presentation marks**.

Controversy

There was a change in the marking system from 2003 after controversy in the pairs competition at the 2002 Olympic Games. Russian pair Elena Berezhnaya and Anton Sikharulidze had made a couple of mistakes in their free skate, but Canadians Jamie Salé and David Pelletier skated perfectly. However, five of the nine judges marked the Russians higher, so they won gold. The Canadian team appealed after the French judge admitted she had been pressured into changing her decision by Russian officials. In the end, both pairs were given gold—but a change in judging was clearly needed.

The Russian and Canadian pairs pose with their gold medals following a successful Canadian appeal.

The new rules

Following the controversy in 2002, programs are now marked out of 10 rather than 6. For the technical mark, each element—such as a type of jump—is given a value, and the nine judges give their mark depending on how well the element is performed. For the presentation mark, judges look at factors such as choreography, timing, and interpretation of the music. The marks are added together, and the skater or skaters with the most points win.

NO WAY!

South Korea's Yu-Na Kim set a points record for women in the Vancouver Winter Olympics in 2010. She finished 23 points ahead of the second-place competitor.

The area where skaters wait for their marks is known as the kiss and cry. This is because skaters usually do one or the other of these things, depending on how good their marks are!

PREPARING FOR COMPETITIONS

Preparing for a major international competition is hard work. These are just some of the things professional skaters need to think about.

Music

Music is the first thing that skaters have to decide on. Sometimes skaters might build a routine around music, or they might choose a theme or emotion and then look for music to match. Either way, the choice of music can make or break a skater's season.

Choreography

Each year, skaters have to create new routines and challenge themselves to increase the difficulty. Choreography is the sequence of elements that make up a skater's routine. It is closely linked to the music. Coaches often help with choreographing, and sometimes other people may be brought in to give some new ideas.

A great finishing pose can leave a lasting impression on the judges.

Costumes can really help to set the mood for a dance.

Costumes

The costumes worn by competitors are important, too. They have to enhance the music and the choreography, but not distract from it. Certain styles of costume will suit particular pieces of music. Many skaters hire costume designers to help them.

NO WAY!

When Torvill and Dean decided to use Ravel's *Boléro* for their routine, they had to shorten it to fit into the maximum time allowed. However, they could not quite get it short enough without losing the feel of the music. The solution? To stay kneeling on the ice for the first 18 seconds. The clock starts only when the couple starts to skate. However, new rules now prevent posing at the beginning of a routine.

MAJOR EVENTS

There are a number of different international competitions for skating, in addition to national and local events. The Winter Olympics comes around once every four years and is the main tournament for most skaters. There are five medals available: men's singles, women's singles, pairs, ice dance, and a new team event for the 2014 Winter Olympics in Sochi, Russia. Each team will include six skaters: one man, one woman, a pair, and an ice dance couple. Each individual, pair, or couple will be given points for their routines, and the team with the most points wins the gold medal.

When complete, the Iceberg Skating Palace in Sochi, Russia, will hold 12,000 spectators for the Winter Olympics in 2014.

NO WAY!

Tara Lipinski won gold for the United States in the 1998 Olympic Ladies' Singles competition at the age of 15. She is the youngest-ever winner of a Winter Olympic gold medal.

NAIL-BITING MOMENT!

Zhang Dan and Zhang Dao were in second place after the short program in the pairs competition at the 2006 Winter Olympics. During their free skate, they attempted a throw quad salchow, where the man throws the woman and she performs a quadruple salchow. Dan ended up crashing into the boards around the edge of the ice. Everyone waited to see what would happen as she was helped off the ice. Many thought that the couple's competition was over, but they came back onto the ice and skated well enough to win silver.

Qualifying

Qualification places are gained by accumulating points at the World Championships in the year before the Olympics. The higher the country's skaters rank in that competition, the more points are gained. Skaters can also qualify by placing well at the competition named by the International Skating Union as a qualification event.

American skating star Michelle Kwan gathers flowers and gifts thrown onto the ice by spectators.

World Championships

The Figure Skating World Championships take place every year. The top 200 skaters from up to 50 countries take part in the four disciplines: women's, men's, pairs, and ice dance. The result of the final World Championships before an Olympic year affects how many skaters each country may send to the Olympics.

Junior events

Junior World Championships and Grand Prix events also take place. Skaters must be between the ages of 13 and 19 (or 21 for men in the pairs or ice dance disciplines).

American ice dancers Meryl Davis and Charlie White (center) won gold at the 2011 World Championships.

Other competitions

The U.S. Figure Skating Championships are held once a year to determine the champions of the United States. The event also counts toward qualifying for the World and Four Continents Championships. For skaters from the Americas, Asia, Oceania, and Africa, the Four Continents Championships takes place once a year. The annual European Figure Skating Championships are for the top skaters in Europe.

The World Team Trophy began in 2009 and is similar to the new Olympic team event, but two skaters for the men's and women's individual disciplines compete, instead of one.

British pair Penny Coomes and Nick Buckland perform at the European Championships in 2012.

NO WAY!

In January 1994, Nancy Kerrigan was attacked and hit in the knee while training for the U.S. National Championships. She was unable to compete. Tonya Harding, a rival of Kerrigan's, went on to win. Later, it came out that Harding's ex-husband organized the attack. Harding said she knew nothing about the attack and, although many did not believe her, she was allowed to compete in the Olympics. Watched by 120 million people, Kerrigan won silver, while Harding finished only eighth. Harding was later banned from figure skating for life because of her involvement with the scandal.

SKATING FOR FUN

Skating is not just for Olympic hopefuls or professional skaters. It is an enjoyable pastime that anyone can do. It is also great exercise!

Christmas skating

Ice skating is one of the traditional activities in New York, Chicago, London, and many other cities around the world during the winter. New York has a number of rinks set up at landmarks around the city, such as Central Park, Rockefeller Center, and Citi Pond at Bryant Park. Rinks usually open from the end of October through the end of February. Skating sessions take place through the day and often into the night as people celebrate the holiday season.

Somerset House in London is famous for its winter ice rink.

Indoor ice rinks

Skating isn't just for cold weather, though. Indoor ice rinks are usually open throughout the year, and they often have figure skating clubs you can join. You can find all the information you need on the U.S. Figure Skating Association's web site (see page 46).

NO WAY!

In 1876, the first artificial skating rink was built in London. It was called the Glaciarium.

WARNING!

If it gets really cold, it can sometimes be safe to skate outside on a pond or small lake. However, before you do so, you must always make sure that the ice is thick enough and safe enough to hold your weight. Bait stores and resorts near lakes should be able to give advice.

Skating is lots of fun for all the family!

Watching figure skating

The obvious place to watch ice skating is at competitions—either locally or at major championships. Professional ice shows such as Stars on Ice also tour the country regularly and often include figure skaters who have gone professional or are in between competitions.. These professional ice shows came into existence after top skaters made their reputations in ice shows set up by skating clubs around the United States during the 1920s and 1930s.

"Doing shows is always a side of skating that I've loved, it's the performing. I get to do that without the pressure..."

– Kurt Browning

Skating audiences can be very passionate in support of their favorite skaters!

Competition galas

If tickets to a major competition are difficult to buy, another option is to see the gala that takes place at the end of the competition. The galas feature competitors performing more relaxed routines that do not have any required elements—they are just skaters having fun. Some amazing routines have been seen over the years, along with some fantastic costumes!

A gala is an opportunity to have fun without the pressure of competition.

Stars on Ice

Stars on Ice was created by American figure skating star and Olympic gold medalist Scott Hamilton in 1986. The following year, the show was shown on television for the first time, and it has since gone on to win Emmy Awards. Top stars join the show regularly, allowing audience members to see their favorite skaters outside of the rules and regulations of competition. In 2012, Evan Lysacek, Sasha Cohen, and Kurt Browning all performed.

Learning to skate

Skating helps to keep you fit and improve your posture and balance. It is also a lot of fun. If you are interested in learning to skate, it is worth taking some classes. Your local ice rink will probably have group lessons available, and you can usually rent skates.

The Figure Skating Basic Skills Program is the learn-to-skate program of U.S. Figure Skating. Group lessons are available in hundreds of facilities throughout the country. Certificates of achievement can be gained as a skater passes each level of skating.

CAROLINA KOSTNER

Born: February 8, 1987, in Bolzano, Italy
Nationality: Italian
Started skating: 1990
Practice during skating season: 48 hours a week
Job: Student
Known for: Being the first Italian woman to win the World Championships (in 2012)
Interesting fact: Carolina's favorite actor is Johnny Depp.

Skating associations

The International Skating Union is the main international association. It has 50 member nations. It decides the **rules of conduct** and what required elements must be included in competitions. Many countries have their own national governing bodies, too.

Why is skating such a fascinating sport?

Figure skating is a good sport to watch and try. Watching as a professional skater lands a complicated jump can take your breath away. Seeing skaters from your country win at international events such as the Olympics can fill you with national pride. If you enjoy watching figure skating live or on television, why not try it yourself?

Spectacular routines full of jumps and spins mean that figure skating is one of the greatest shows you can see.

QUIZ

How much do you know about figure skating? Do you know your toe loop from your camel spin? Find out by answering these questions!

1. Why was a new marking system introduced in 2004?

a) The judges got bored of handing out the same marks over and over.

b) A judging scandal caused the change.

c) A group of top skaters decided they wanted marks out of 10 not 6.

2. What was the name of the first artificial ice rink?

a) Glaciarium

b) Londinium

c) Icerinkium

3. How old was Tara Lipinski when she won the Olympics?

a) 25

b) 12

c) 15

4. When were compulsory figures removed from major competitions?

a) 1890

b) 2012

c) 1990

5. In ice dancing, what's the maximum length of time that a long lift can last for?

a) 2 minutes

b) 12 seconds

c) 30 seconds

6. What were the first skates made of?

a) the leg bones of animals

b) plastic

c) soil

7. What is a camel spin?

a) a spin performed while seated on top of a camel

b) a spin performed with both legs parallel to the ice

c) a spin performed with one leg parallel to the ice

8. How many countries belong to the International Skating Union?

a) 50

b) 250

c) 2

7–8 correct answers: Clearly, you know your stuff when it comes to figure skating! Perhaps you could be competing for medals in the future.

4–6 correct answers: Not bad. Try to find an ice rink in your area and get some practice in.

1–3 correct answers: Try to watch some skating on television or on the Internet and see if you can learn more about it. Maybe even give it a try?

Answers

1. b
2. a
3. c
4. c
5. b
6. a
7. c
8. a

GLOSSARY

artistry creative ability

axel jump jump in which the skater takes off from his or her forward outside edge and lands on the back outside edge of the opposite foot. A single axel includes 1.5 revolutions. The jump is named after Norwegian figure skater Axel Paulsen (1855–1938).

choreography sequence of steps and movements

combination when one element is closely followed by another, such as a jump followed by a spin

discipline type of activity. Ice dance is a discipline within the sport of figure skating.

edges two sides of the blade on a skate. The blade is curved front to back and side to side, so there are eight possible edges from which to skate. The inside edge is the edge on the inner side of the leg; the outside edge is on the outside of the leg. There is also a forward edge and a backward edge for each side and each edge.

element particular move such as a triple lutz jump

flip jump toe-pick-assisted jump, in which the skater takes off from the back inside edge of one foot and lands on the back outside edge of the other foot

free skate routine that follows the short program for singles and pairs. The choreography is meant to show off the skater's technical and artistic skills.

inside edge *see* edges

lift in pairs skating and ice dance, movement in which one of the partners (usually the woman) is lifted, held in position, and then set down on the ice. In pairs, the man has his arms extended above his head, but there are height restrictions for ice dance.

loop jump edge jump, where the skater takes off from a back outside edge and lands on the same back outside edge

lutz jump toe-pick-assisted jump, in which the skater glides backward and takes off from the back outside edge of one foot. He or she lands on the back outside edge of the other foot. The jump is named after Austrian figure skater Alois Lutz (1898–1918).

44

outside edge *see* edges

pioneer be the first to do something

posture way that someone holds his or her body

presentation mark mark given to skaters relating to how they performed, including speed, variation, use of space, and expression of the music. This used to be called the artistic impression mark.

required element one of the moves that has to be included in every competitor's program

rules of conduct set of expectations and ways of behaving that apply to everyone who plays a particular sport

salchow an edge jump, where the skater takes off from the back inside edge of one foot and lands on the back outside edge of the other foot. The jump is named after Swedish figure skater Ulrich Salchow (1877–1949).

short program first routine that is performed by singles and pairs in a competition. Eight required elements have to be performed by all competitors.

sit spin spin performed in a sitting position, with the upper part of the skating leg parallel to the ice

spiral performed on one leg, with the non-skating leg lifted above hip height

synchronized skating when a team of 12 to 20 skaters performs as one on the ice at the same time

technical merit marks based on the difficulty, variety, and speed of a performance

throw jump in pairs skating, when the woman is thrown in the air by the man and lands without assistance on a back outside edge. The throw can include up to four revolutions.

toe loop jump in a toe-pick-assisted jump, the skater takes off from his or her back outside edge. He or she then lands on that same edge.

toe pick jagged teeth on the front of a skate's blade. The toe pick is used in takeoff for some jumps and as the pivot point for spins.

turnout rotation of the legs from the hip sockets

unison performing at the same time

FIND OUT MORE

Books

Claybourne, Anna. *Ice Dancing* (On the Radar: Dance). Minneapolis: Lerner, 2012.

Gustaitis, Joseph. *Figure Skating* (Winter Olympic Sports). New York: Crabtree, 2010.

Hines, James R. *The Historical Dictionary of Figure Skating*. Lanham, MD.: Scarecrow, 2011.

Hunter, Nick. *The Winter Olympics*. Chicago: Heinemann Library, 2014.

Web sites

www.isu.org
This is the International Skating Union's web site.

www.olympic.org/figure-skating
The Olympic web site has lots of photos and videos about four main figure skating disciplines.

www.usfsa.org
The U.S. Figure Skating Association's web site has everything you need to know about ice skating in the United States.

Topics to research

- See what you can find out about the Winter Olympics, particularly how it became a separate competition from the Summer Olympics.

- Find out more about some of ice skating's rivalries over the years, from Yu Na Kim and Mao Asada to Brian Boitano and Brian Orser.

- Some people think that figure skating, and ice dancing in particular, is not a "sport." Discover why they think this and decide for yourself: Is figure skating a sport? Explain your decision.

INDEX

axels 17, 20

Biellmann spins 19
blades 10
boots 10
Browning, Kurt 17, 38

camel spins 18
Chan, Patrick 14, 24
choreography 25, 27, 29, 30
Christmas skating 36
clothing 11
competitions 32–35, 38
compulsory figures 25
controversies 28
core strength 12
cost of training 14
costumes 31, 39
Cousins, Robin 13

Dean, Christopher 4, 31, 39
death spirals 22
diet, healthy 13
disciplines 5
dizziness 19
drapes 23

edge jumps 17
equipment 10–11
European Figure Skating Championships 35

flexibility 12, 23
flips 16
free skate 4, 15, 19, 24, 25, 27
fun, skating for 36–37

galas 39

Han, Cong 23
Harding, Tonya 35
history of skating 6–9

ice dance 26, 27, 39
ice rinks 11, 36, 37, 40
International Skating Union (ISU) 9, 41

jumps 16–17, 20
junior events 34

Kerr, Sinead and John 21
Kerrigan, Nancy 35
Kim, Yu-Na 25, 29
Kostner, Carolina 40

lakes and rivers, skating on 37
layback spins 18, 19
learning to skate 40
lifts 21, 27
Lipinski, Tara 32
loops 17
lutz 16

marking 28–29
mental preparation 15
Muir, Scott 11
music 25, 27, 29, 30, 31

Olympics see Winter Olympics

pairs 26–27
pairs lifts 21
plyometrics 12
preparing for competitions 30–31
presentation marks 28, 29

professional ice shows 38
pull-throughs 23

salchows 17, 33
Savchenko, Aliona 26
short program 24, 27
singles 24–25
sit spins 18
skates 6, 10
spins 12, 18–19
spirals 22
Stars on Ice 39
Sui, Wenjing 23
synchronized skating 5
Szolkowy, Robin 26

team competitions 5
technical merit 28, 29
throws 20, 33
toe jumps 16
toe loops 16, 17
toe pick 10, 16
Torvill, Jayne 4, 31, 39
training 4, 12–15
twist lifts 20

unison 22, 26
upright spins 18
U.S. Figure Skating Championships 35

Virtue, Tessa 11

Wagner, Ashley 15
watching figure skating 38–39, 41
Winter Olympics 4, 9, 19, 25, 27, 28, 29, 32, 33
Witt, Katarina 5, 19
World Championships 9, 13, 21, 33, 34